Teja's Day At The Aquarium

written by Teja Harper

illustrated by Carolyn Vaughan

Copyright © 2022 Teja Harper

ISBN: 978-0-578-36712-5

All rights reserved. No part of this work covered by the copyright hereon may be reproduced in print or electronically without the written permission of the author.

Printed in the U.S.A.

This book is dedicated to all the children around the world
by promoting childhood reading
to help engage children in reading activities.

Hi! My name is Teja and I'm 10 years old. I enjoy outings with my Dad, Mom and little brother. We get to experience new places together. Let us take you on the journey, as I love to get out and do fun things with my family.

Thank you for reading.

Teja loves fish, so when she and her family went to the aquarium she was very excited!

The first fish Teja saw at the aquarium were Red Garra, also known as Dr. Fish. When she put her hands in the fish tank, lots of little fish crowd around her hand, as they cleaned the skin.

Teja laughs from the tingles of the fish. "Is that why they are called Dr. Fish, Daddy?" Teja says, "Yes, that's correct Teja," dad says.

Teja saw the shrimp next,
they clean fingernails.

When she put her hand in the shrimp tank,
they nibbled around her fingernails.

"It tickles", said Teja as she giggled.

As they walked further, Teja and her family saw the otters splashing water, swimming and playing with each other.

"Look Daddy, they splash like TJ" Teja said excitedly while holding her little brother's hand.

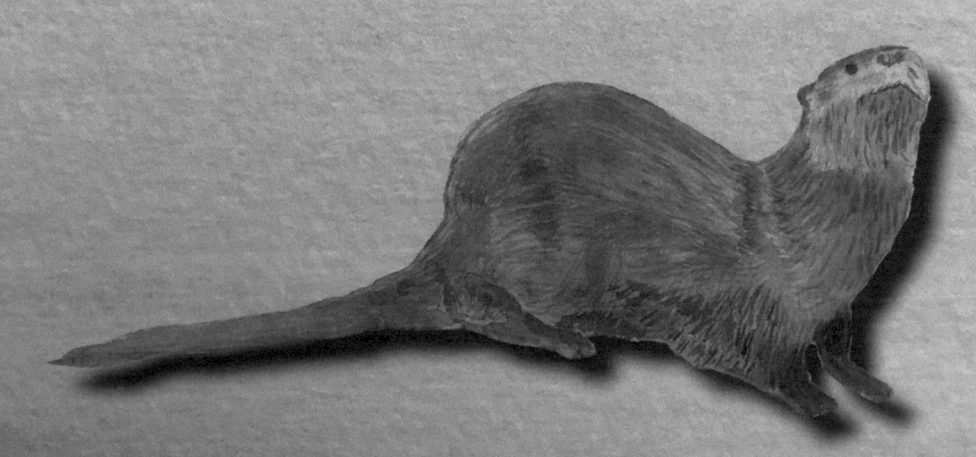

We saw turtles in all different sizes, small, medium and large. "Mommy, Mommy" Teja says smiling, "Did you know turtles are good at swimming?" "Yes" says Mommy.

"And also hiding" Teja says, as the largest turtle swam away.

"Jelly fish are one of the most beautiful fish in the world TJ," Teja said, as she held her little brother up to look at the tank.

"There are many colors of jellyfish, some are translucent, meaning you can see through them" Dad says.

"And they look like umbrellas," Teja says laughing!

The family continued walking through the aquarium, passing the clown fish.
"They look cool" Teja said.

Clown fish live in groups call schools.

Teja's favorite part was feeding the stingrays. touching them gently,

"WOW! these are slimy" she said.

Looking into the big fish tank was so relaxing.

Teja and her family sat there enjoying
the sharks, stingray, and moon fish
as they swam by.

There was a Goliath grouper fish who swam at the bottom of the fish tank.

"Look, Look!," Teja says to TJ, "That's a huge fish!"

Looking at the tank, TJ starts smiling.

The last tank they passed was the Octopus.

"Can you see the octopus kids?"
Dad says to Teja and TJ.

Looking very hard into the tank, Teja found the octopus, "I found it daddy, I found it" jumping up and down excited, Teja said.

"Good Job Princess", Dad says,
"they are good at blending in with their environment, this is called camouflage."

While leaving the aquarium we passed a lemonade stand.

"Can we please get some lemonade Mommy?"
"Of course we can" says Mom as they walk out of the exit door.

After taking her first drink, Teja smiles.

"This is the BEST DAY EVER!", she says, while looking back at the Aquarium.

Stay tuned for other adventures with
Teja and her family!

The author, Teja Harper, is 10 yrs old. She loves spending time with her family & friends. She is planning to be a dentist when she grows up. For now she enjoys swimming, running track and playing with her little brother TJ.

She is extremely proud to be an author at such a young age, and is encouraged by her parents to continue to dream BIG.

The illustrator, Carolyn Vaughan, is a thoughtful book designer and artist currently living in St. Louis, MO with her husband and cat, Emmy. She is accepting commissions for book designs and art (landscapes, pet portraits, etc.).

You can find out more about her work and see examples at cvaughandesigns.com.

www.ingramcontent.com/pod-product-compliance
Lightning Source LLC
Chambersburg PA
CBHW041325290426

44109CB00004B/128